Chapter 1: What is Industry Consolidation?

Consolidation is simply the merger and amalgamation of many companies in one industry into fewer larger corporations. Industry consolidation generally takes place when an industry is in a **mature phase and a small number of companies control the majority of the market share**.

Consolidation takes place after any industries organic growth has slowed or begun its decline. Companies' merge with one another to achieve investment synergies cut down on cuts and achieve more efficient operations. Consolidation is a normal part of any industry. It drives down the cost of goods and services and make the marketplace more competitive and affordable – for consumers.

Industry consolidation is almost inevitable: over time, most industries will consolidate to where the largest two or three companies will dominate an industry and the rest of the smaller players are rendered almost. Think about the world's largest companies- they generally operate as near monopolies in mature industries. These companies all started out in industries with thousands of competitors. As industries matured, competitors were eliminated or bought out by larger companies. The process of consolidation may take many decades, but is generally a predictable part of the business cycle.

Largest 5 companies in the world by Market capitalization (2018)

- Apple
- Amazon
- Google
- Microsoft
- Tencent

As you can see, these companies all have extremely dominant positions in their respective industries. It's difficult to imagine these companies being dethroned any time soon, they simply have such strong competitive advantages and are far, far ahead of any competition at this point.

"The key to investing is not assessing how much an industry is going to affect society, or how much it will grow, but rather determining the competitive advantage of any given company and, above all, the durability of that advantage."

Warren Buffett

Chapter 2: Why Industry Consolidation is needed

Industry consolidation is often viewed in a negative light. Left-wing magazines and liberals generally scorn at the thought of dominant companies increasing their market share and supposedly limiting the amount of choice that consumers have. This is simply false. **Industry consolidation is a logical part of maximizing efficiency and eliminating wastage across a sector.** The popular perception in the media, is that competition is something which is an ingrained part of capitalism and an integral component of the market system. However, the reality is that pure competition creates inefficiencies and hurts profit margins. If there is a small corporate pie and a larger number of companies who battle one another to obtain their slice, firms often resort to price wars and engage in a race to the bottom. This simply drives most companies out of business until a process of consolidation takes place.

Let us take the American oil refineries as an example. Back When John Rockefeller was forming the famous Standard Oil Trust, he was constantly frustrated because new oil refineries begun popping up every two weeks. Rockefeller was busily buying out almost every single refiner in Cleveland, who tried to compete with him on pricing or by earning exclusive geographic contracts. Predictably, most of these companies that popped up ultimately ended up failing or being forcefully acquired by the Standard Oil Trust.

The massive consolidation which took place allowed Standard Oil to acquire huge advantages of scale which allowed them to become the low cost oil producers and control a massive amount of the world's oil. Needless to say, Rockefeller also negotiated viciously with railroads to obtain massive cost advantages which ultimately pushed competitors out of business. Ironically, the biggest casualties of the Standard Oil Trust were the companies that tried to compete directly with Rockefeller- practically all the competition went out of business. **Consumers on the other hand, received extremely low prices and excellent service.**

Currently, the number of operating oil refineries has consistently fallen. There were previously 254 oil refineries in 1982 and now there are just 137 in 2011. However, the operating capacity of today's 137 facilities is over 830,000 barrels per day more than it was in 1982. What this means, is that today's refineries have a greater market share than they had previously, while capacity has increased, meaning that there are more profits to go around. Consolidation in oil refining has been absolutely necessary, as there are massive capital expenditures associated with entering the industry and equally high maintenance costs. **Consolidation has rationalized the industry and made profit margins more stable for the remaining firms.** Without consolidation, we would simply have watched hundreds of refineries go out of business.

Another, more recent example of industry consolidation is the American airlines. The passenger airline industry had over 20 large national network airlines just 15-20 years ago. There were hundreds of airline bankruptcies and massive employee layoffs as companies seemed to compete exclusive on price. Vicious competition left the industry decimated and created constant chaos, strikes and conflict as nobody was a winner.

The industry is now dominated by just four airlines (United, Delta, American, and Southwest), each having their own hubs that limit competition in major markets. Employees have safer jobs, profit margins are up and the industry is operating in a much healthier manner. **Rationalization of the airline industry was the only way to achieve sustainability.**

On a smaller scale, in companies which I have owned, that the clients received the greatest amount of value, were the companies that competed in the least competitive space. It is clear that if a company is not required to expend all of its energy fighting competition; it is much simpler to focus on providing your clients the best possible service.

How consolidation benefits all

1) **Access to better benefits and compensation for employees**

One of the primary competitive advantages of mergers and acquisitions is that companies can eliminate redundant employees. Yes, this is painful as some employees lose their jobs, however for employees that that stay on, there is more money to go around. Benefits can be increased and employees can receive much better pay. Offering higher wages and better benefits also helps to create high quality, desirable jobs, and the type of employment society needs.

2) **Productivity increases**

As industries become more consolidated, individual companies become more profitable. This is because they don't face as much competition, which almost inevitably drives down costs and allows for rational pricing. Additionally, as companies generate more revenue due to less competition, they can reinvest to boost worker productivity.

3) **Operating leverage by growing the top line**

Fixed costs are costs which remain unchanged irrespective of business performance. These costs are usually incurred regardless of the amount of production which the business undertakes. Fixed costs & variable costs comprise the total costs of the company, which is the amount that the firm must earn to break-even.

As companies grow their market share, fixed costs generally remain relatively stable, which means that increased sales can go primarily to the bottom line.

4) **Consolidated firms can fight against inflation**

Inflation takes place when there is a constant increase in the cost of goods. This has been known to negatively impact businesses very negatively. In a consolidated industry, businesses can pass on increased prices to consumers. This prevents margin erosion and allows ongoing industry stability.

5) **Capital allocation: Firms in consolidated industries can engage in share repurchases and pay dividends, providing value to their investors.**

Share repurchases are transactions in which a company buys back its own common stock. This a common way of returning value to stockholders, as a lower number of shares outstanding results in higher earnings per share for remaining shareholders. Share repurchases also increase the book value (net equity) per share.

Dividends (cash payments by the firm to their shareholders can be paid out in mature industries to investors for a number of reasons.

- *The firm is not able to reinvest all of its earnings.* When a firm is in its initial phase of growth, the company usually requires as **much capital as it can** get to grow the business. Companies then reinvest earnings back into the business to further grow and expand into the future. However, once companies reach maturity, this is no required. An example of this would be firms such as Apple or Coca-Cola who have grown to the point that they have excess funds and don't need all the money they have to grow the company. As a consequence these firms pay dividends.
- *Stability*: Firms who are able to pay dividends usually have stable earnings which have grown over time and continue to trend upward.

The number one idea is to view a stock as an ownership of the business and to judge the staying quality of the business in terms of its competitive advantage. Look for more value in terms of discounted future cash-flow than you are paying for. Move only when you have an advantage.

Charles T Munger

Chapter 3: How Industries evolve over time

Industries evolve in a predictable manner. There are generally four stages of development:

- **Opening:** An industry is in the early stage of development and there is massive opportunity to earn money, scale and capture the market. There is a near free-for all entry into the market as companies try to capture what they can.
- **Scale:** Companies who succeed begin to focus on profitability and increasing their market share as they realize they need economies of scale, either to displace incumbents or to effectively capture enough consumers.
- **Focus:** Companies go after an established section of the market, rather than just trying to enter. Specialization occurs when companies begin refining their offerings and evaluating where they can make the most money.
- **Maturity (Alliances):** As soon as growth begins to slow or decline, companies begin to form alliances and consolidate their market share. At this point, profitability margins are usually at their highest point and competition at its lowest. I recommend trying to focus on investing in firms who are at stages 2-4 in the development cycle, while avoiding those in the opening stage.

How long does it take for an industry to evolve?

Doesn't matter. Some industries can reach maturity very quickly, whilst others may take more than 25 years. The most important thing is simply that you understand at what stage an industry is at.

What companies should do at each stage

Opening: Aggressively build on their first-mover advantages by scaling up the business, achieving economies of scale and establishing barriers of entry which make it difficult for new entrants to compete. At this stage it is most important that companies focus on increasing their revenue and gain market share, rather than worrying about profits.

Scale: This stage is all about building scale. Major players begin to emerge, buying up competitors and forming empires. The top three players in a stage 2 industry will own 15% to 45% of their market, as the industry consolidates rapidly.

Focus: Companies focus on expanding their core business and continuing to aggressively outgrow the competition. The goal is to emerge as a powerhouse. You can attack underperformers aggressively, decide whether to crush or acquire start-ups.

The well-entrenched competition at this phase will attack underperformers. Recognizing start-up competitors early on allows focus-stage competitors to decide whether to crush them, acquire them, or simply emulate them. Stage 3 companies should also identify other major players that will likely survive into the next, and final, stage and avoid all-out assaults.

Stage 4: Balance and Alliance. Here the titans of industry reign, from tobacco to soft drinks to defense. The industry concentration rate can reach as much as 70% to 90% of the market. Large companies may form alliances with their peers because growth is now more challenging. Companies don't move through stage 4; they stay in it. Thus, firms in these industries must defend their leading positions. They must find new ways to grow their core business in a mature industry and create a new wave of growth by spinning off new businesses into industries in early stages of consolidation. They must be alert to the potential for industry regulation and the danger of being lulled into complacency by their own dominance.

Your job as an investor is to recognize what stage the company is at in the consolidation cycle and ultimately make an investment if you believe that it can become one of the industry titans. As a business owner, it is essential that you realize what stage your company is at in the industry and aim to scale and become the dominant player in your industry.

"It is not necessary to do extraordinary things to get extraordinary results."

Warren Buffett

Chapter 4: Industry Consolidation: Providing you with certain investment returns

Any time you put money at risk in an attempt to profit; there is a level of uncertainty. Uncertainty is the **inability to forecast future events. However, this is not risk.** People can't predict the extent of a possible recession, when it's going to start/end, how much it will cost, or what companies will be able to make it through unscathed. Most companies normally predict sales and production trends for the investing public to follow assuming normal market conditions.

Investing in a company that operates in a consolidated industry clearly decreases the level of uncertainty. It is far easier to predict how a dominant company will **perform in a consolidated industry, compared to a growing firm in a sector that is just starting out**. The company may go through tough times; however it is easy to predict that companies which dominate a sector will often come out of challenging times stronger than ever. In fact, tough times in an industry can help a dominant company to further consolidate their industry leads.

Risk in Investing

Risk is a poorly understood concept in investment. The vast majority of investors believe that risk can be mitigated by wide diversification; they believe that holding hundreds or even thousands of different securities is the way to protect themselves. Investing in firms that operate in consolidated industries however, mitigates **the vast majority of the risk** involved with investing in a company.

Risk arises as a result of something improbable or unforeseeable having taken place which causes you as an investor to loose capital permanently. Risk is also opportunity cost, the risk of achieving an inadequate return compared to having invested capital else.

Let us now evaluate the potential sources of risk:

- The risk of not know what you are doing.
- Total number of decision-making factors.
- The nature of the financial asset.
- The price paid for the financial asset.
- The risk of an incorrect judgement of the future.

If you invest in strong companies that operate largely in consolidated industries, you can greatly reduce the number of uncertainties and errors you may might- vastly decreasing risk. The point of this book, is to show you how you can largely mitigate risk by investing in a consolidated industry, particularly if you able to correctly value the underlying financial asset.

Chapter 5: Competitive advantage: How a business in a consolidated industry can grow profits over time

A business in a consolidated industry can build upon its competitive advantage. A competitive advantage is the reason which the business has thrived in the first place. Once an industry begins consolidating, the business can continue to build upon this advantage and solidify its leadership even further.

Competitive advantages can take a variety of forms depending on the type of company which has been setup and what sector it operates in.

- **A company can own a powerful brand**, which means that consumers would be willing to pay more for their brands. Or the company's products might be protected by **patents, as is** in the case of pharmaceutical companies, granting them a monopoly for the duration of the patent.
- **Switching costs** are another type of competitive advantage which arise when the benefits of changing one company's product for another are outweighed by the costs involved for the client in doing so. For example, people can be quite reluctant to switch banks, even if the bank next door is offering the same or better conditions, because changing banks can be a very cumbersome process (due to paperwork and changing direct debits, etc.). Nine times out of ten, the hassle is more than it's worth for the client.
- **Network advantages** can also exist, as in the case of Facebook. Here the value of the service provided by the network increases with the number of people who use it. A social network can be the best in the world but it will be of little value if it only has one user.
- We maintain that one of the easiest ways to obtain a strong competitive advantage is to do something which **nobody else wants to do**. Morticians and cigarette manufacturers would be examples of occupations and businesses which benefit from a strong competitive advantage, namely that their business is abhorrent to many people and entrepreneurs. Similarly, we see a near complete consensus that the newspaper business is dead in the long run. If a company is out of favour, fits our other seven criteria and maintains a strong competitive advantage, we're interested.
- **Scale**- a way to generate a competitive advantage **is to be in a business that requires massive size**. Think of the duopoly shared by The Boeing Company (NYSE:BA) and Airbus. Who else do you know building commercial airliners these days? Every 10 to 15 years they have to commit billions of dollars of capital to design and build airplanes which won't exist for years. We contend that this massive capital outlay prevents anybody new from emerging as a major aircraft manufacturer. Pharmaceuticals and biotech are other industries which require large scale, but do not face the same cyclicality as airlines. It takes about one billion dollars of capital (on average) to create a blockbuster drug and immense manufacturing and distribution capabilities to sell it around the world.
- A third way we believe you can strengthen your competitive advantage **or widen your moat is to go through tough times in the industry.**

Commodity product selling companies

If a company is selling a commodity style product, there is no question that the most important factor is price. People will never pay more for basic everyday items like oil, insurance or cigarettes than required. Cost advantages, which are enjoyed by companies which have cheaper processes than the competition.

Cost advantages can also come from having a larger scale than the competition. The classic example is the North American supermarket chain, Walmart. Its huge size enables them to be much more efficient in distribution and gives them a strong bargaining power with suppliers. And why are competitive advantages in a consolidated sector so important?

Because without them, companies which generate high returns on capital employed (and this are the ones we like!), attract competitors who are seduced by these high returns. **High returns are of little use if in a few months or years someone detects the business opportunity and copies it.** In Buffett's own words, if you have a fantastic castle (company), it is going to be continually under siege from enemies trying to take it away from you. So the best thing is for the castle to have a deep moat that defends it, in an industry with limited competition.

As asset managers and analysts our job is not just to find companies with competitive advantages but to be constantly monitoring whether these advantages remain valid, keeping track of technological changes, new competitors, etc, which could "attack our castle".

Chapter 6: Return on Equity: How to find the ultimate business

If you have ever heard about Warren Buffett and the writings of Benjamin Graham, you may be familiar with the concept of the **"Margin of Safety"**. That would be, buying something for so much less than it is worth. In the case of monopoly businesses, you have already learnt that the risk is reduced. **Now let's take a look at how a company's return on equity impacts its valuation and how to find the ultimate businesses.**

How Quality *and* Valuation Impact Margin of Safety

The margin of safety can be derived from the gap between price and value, and it can also be derived from the quality of the business. **The latter point is really part of the former...** For example, a business that can steadily grow intrinsic value at a rate of say 12% annually is worth much more than a business that is growing its value at say 4% annually. Since the higher quality compounder is worth more than the lower quality business, the quality compounder offers a larger margin of safety.

Too often, value investors get enticed by cheap metrics and seemingly large discounts between price and value in businesses with shrinking intrinsic value. The problem in these types of cigar butts is that the margin of safety (gap between purchase price and value) is largest the day of the investment. Every day thereafter the business value slowly erodes further, making the investment a race against time.

Buffett's 1987 Roster

In the 1987 annual letter, Buffett mentions that Berkshire's seven largest non-financial subsidiary companies made $180 million of operating earnings and $100 million after tax earnings. But, he says **"by itself, this figure says nothing about economic performance. To evaluate that, we must know how much total capital – debt and equity – was needed to produce these earnings."**

So Buffett was interested in return on invested capital. He goes on to state that these seven business units used virtually no debt, incurring just $2 million of total combined interest charges in 1987, so virtually all capital employed to produce those earnings was equity capital. And these 7 businesses had a combined equity of only $175 million.

So Berkshire had seven businesses that combined to produce the following numbers:

- $178 million pre-tax earnings
- $100 million after tax earnings
- $175 equity capital
- 57% ROE
- 102% Pre-tax ROE

So Buffett's top 7 non-financial businesses produced fabulously high returns on equity with very little use of debt. In short, they were outstanding businesses. Buffett proudly goes on to say that **"You'll seldom see such a percentage anywhere, let alone at large, diversified companies** with nominal leverage." Of course, investor returns depend on price paid in relation to value received, and we are only discussing the value received part of the equation here.

Buffett then voices his opinion on the importance of predictability and stability in business models:

> Experience, however, indicates that the best business returns are usually achieved by companies that are doing something quite similar today to what they were doing five or ten years ago. That is no argument for managerial complacency. Businesses always have opportunities to improve service, product lines, manufacturing techniques, and the like, and obviously these opportunities should be seized. But a business that constantly encounters major change also encounters many chances for major error. Furthermore, economic terrain that is forever shifting violently is ground on which it is difficult to build a fortress-like business franchise. Such a franchise is usually the key to sustained high returns.

Source: Berkshire 1987 Annual Report

But how to find these businesses? Buffett again provides some ideas:

> Second, except for one company that is "high-tech" and several others that manufacture ethical drugs, the companies are in businesses that, on balance, seem rather mundane. Most sell non-sexy products or services in much the same manner as they did ten years ago (though in larger quantities now, or at higher prices, or both). The record of these 25 companies confirms that making the most of an already strong business franchise, or concentrating on a single winning business theme, is what usually produces exceptional economics.

Source: Berkshire 1987 Annual Report

The idea is to locate quality businesses in consolidated industries. And in terms of percentages, there will likely be fewer errors made (fewer permanent capital losses) in the investment compounder. If **you want to reduce unforced errors (reduce losing investments), it helps to get familiar with stable, predictable businesses with long histories of producing above average returns on invested capital.**

You should try to invest in businesses that not only operate in monopoly style industries, but those that earn very high returns on equity. By investing in companies with this profile, you both mitigate your investment risk and maximize your investment gain.

> "Over the long term, it's hard for a stock to earn a much better return that the business which underlies it earns. If the business earns six percent on capital over forty years and you hold it for that forty years, you're not going to make much different than a six percent return - even if you originally buy it at a huge discount. Conversely, if a business earns eighteen percent on capital over twenty or thirty years, even if you pay an expensive looking price, you'll end up with one hell of a result." Charles T Munger

Chapter 7: How to categorize a business

I have always found it useful to correctly categorize a business. You want to know **why** you are making a particular investment and the expectations that you have for a business.

Peter Lynch has six categories which I believe are extremely useful for all of us.

- **Slow Growers**: Large / aging companies growing only slightly faster than the economy as a whole, but often paying regular dividends.
- **Stalwarts**: Large companies that are still able to grow, with annual earnings growth rates of around 10% - 12% (e.g Coca-Cola amp; Procter amp; Gamble).
- **Fast-Growers**: Small, aggressive new firms with annual earnings growth of 20% - 25% a year.
- **Cyclicals**: Companies in which sales and profits tend to rise and fall in somewhat predictable patterns based on the economic cycle (e.g. auto, airline and steel sector).
- **Turnarounds**: Companies that have either pulled themselves out of a serious slump, or got bailed by by the government
- **Asset plays**: Companies where the assets exceed market cap.

Many people have a tendency to believe that industry consolidation takes place only when a business is in a stage of slow and stable growth. While this is theoretically the case, things do not always play out like this in real life. For example, it would be fair to say that Amazon began to consolidate online E-commerce; long before its growth rate began to slow (the company is still on a tear to this day). Similarly, Google dominated search long before it became an industry Stalwart.

My point is that you can find hidden monopolies everywhere. You do not need to wait for an industry to experience 100 years of consolidation to take place. Simply consider the industry dynamics and the company's position relative to competitors. Understand and correctly categorize the business you are looking to invest in, it will help you in making investments. The reason you want to do this is because how much you pay for any financial asset, **depends on the assets quality**. You should absolutely be willing to pay substantially more for a higher quality company.

Chapter 8: Accounting fundamentals

This section is designed to help you refresh your understanding of all of the most important financial metrics. While some of these financials may seem straightforward, it is important that you understand all of these concepts perfectly.

The Balance Sheet

The accounting balance sheet is one of the major financial statements which present a company's financial position at a specific point in time. Analysing the balance sheet is crucial to assessing a company's financial health. A balance sheet can help you to work out your working capital requirements and business liquidity among other measures which provides crucial insight into the state of your business.

A balance sheet has three major components:

- Assets
- Liabilities
- Owner's (Stockholders') Equity

Assets are resources of the company that have been acquired through transactions and have future economic value. Assets on the balance sheet consist of both current and noncurrent assets. Current assets are assets the company expects to convert to cash or use in the business within one year. Noncurrent assets are assets the company estimates it will hold for at least one year. Examples of current assets are cash, accounts receivable, and inventory. Long-term assets are ones the company estimates it will hold for at least one year. Examples of long-term assets are investments and property, plant, and equipment currently in use by the company in day-to-day operations.

A liability is a company's financial debt or obligations. As with assets, these are classified as current or noncurrent. Current liabilities are obligations the company expects to settle within 12 months of the date on the balance sheet. Examples of short term liabilities are: Accounts payable, notes payable, and unearned income. Non-current liabilities are long-term financial obligations listed on a company's balance sheet that are not due a 12 month period. Examples of long term liabilities are: Long term borrowings, deferred tax liabilities and long-term leases

Shareholders' equity is equal to a firm's total assets minus its total liabilities. It is one of the most common financial metrics employed by analysts to determine the financial health of a company. Shareholders' equity represents the net value of a company, or the amount that would be returned to shareholders if all the company's assets were liquidated and all its debts repaid. This is otherwise known as book value. Shareholders' equity is crucial to calculating a number of key accounting metrics, including return on equity, returns on invested capital and operating leverage.

The balance sheet provides important insight into evaluating the financial position of a company at a specific point in time. It is a great starting point for beginning to evaluate a business.

The Income Statement

An income statement is a report that shows a business's total income and expenses for a specific period of time. The income statement an extremely important report as it illustrates exactly how much money a firm is making or losing.

Investors can utilise their income statements to evaluate the breakdown of company earnings/expenses, gross margins, selling and profit margins. Income statements can be compared over a period of time to assess how a business's' prospects are evolving over time and whether or not their financial position is improving.

What does the Income Statement look like?

A sample income statement can be illustrated with the following format:

Total Sales	$942,000
Cost of Sales	$512,000
Gross Income	$430,000
Selling & Administrative expenses	$330,000
Operating Income	$100,000
Other income/expenses	($2000)
Pre-tax Income	$98,000
Taxes	$24,000
Net income after tax	$74,000

As illustrated in the income statement above, a firm's efficiency can be illustrated by their margins in four key sectors:

A firm's gross margin: Generally margins above 40% are outstanding, while below 20% is considered unsustainable. This is a major indicator of the sustainability of the firm's income. In the example above the gross margin is 47%.

A firm's operating income. Above 15% is considered excellent, while below 10% is fragile. In the example above the operating margin is 10.6%.

A firm's pre-tax income: This utilised in conjunction with the operating income will assist in determining how much tax a business pays. This may vary dependent on the nature of their income/structure of the business.

A firm's net income: This is how much income is ultimately attributable to the firm's owners and a key reference point for valuing the business. It is also crucial to calculate a firm's growth by comparing how quickly it has been able to grow its net income over a period of time. In this example, the net profit is $74,000

A comprehensive analysis of a business's income statement can enable an investor to analyse profits margins and profitability ratios. This can then be evaluated over a period of time to see if a company is improving its operating efficiency.

A Businesses' Free Cash Flow

Free Cash Flow, otherwise known as owner's earnings is one of the most important financial metrics used in valuation. It enables a business owner to understand just how much money the business is **actually generating and can distribute to its owners.**

Free Cash flow can be calculated from the cash flow statement by:

(1) Taking reported earnings (net income) adding

(2) Depreciation, depletion & amortization subtracting

(3) The average amount of capital expenditure for plant and equipment, etc. which the business requires to maintain its competitive advantage in the market.

Benefits of calculating Free Cash Flow

Calculating the Free Cash Flow does not enable a business owner to put a precise figure on the total valuation of his or her firm, particularly because (3) is usually an estimate. However it provides a more accurate measure of the real earning power of a firm. This is because net income, often significantly understates or overstates real owner's earnings.

Examples of how Calculating Free Cash Flow reflects earning power

Business which spend significant amounts of money each year to maintain sales volumes or maintain their position in the marketplace, will find that their capital expenditures significantly outweigh their depreciation & amortization costs. In such cases, net income significantly overstates real earnings, as distributing money to owners would impact the long term health of the business. These are considered 'capital intensive' businesses, as they decay rapidly without significant levels of investment.

However, businesses which do not need to spend a significant amount of money to maintain their competitive position will find themselves a virtuous cycle. Significant amounts of money will be generated by the firm and these are free to be distributed to owners or potentially reinvested into new lines of production to grow the business, attract more customers or enter new markets. Businesses which are 'capital light' often tend to increase their profitability strongly over time.

Calculating free cash flow is of enormous help to an owner looking to measure how much his firm is truly worth and evaluating how this evolves over time.

A firm's quality of earnings

Determining a firm's quality of earnings involves evaluating how precise, relevant, comparable and unbiased a company's financial performance is in a given period. There are a number of factors which a business owner can use to judge a firm's performance, including:

- **Consistency of Accounting Standards**: Has the business utilised the same method of accounting throughout its reporting history or has it deviated significantly from quarter to quarter. This includes the methods used to calculate depreciation, inventory, accounts receivable and restructuring charges. A business which deviates significantly from Generally Accepted Accounting Practices or varies how it reports its metrics, may have a lower quality of earnings than initially apparent.
- **Auditor's Report**: Should the accounting firm who audited the company have provided an unqualified opinion this is generally reflective that the firm has been fully compliant with standard accounting practices. Conversely, if a qualified opinion was provided, this means that the auditor encountered a number of situations which did not comply with standard reporting. This may be a warning sign of a lower quality of earnings.
- **Tax rates**: Has the businesses tax rate stayed constant across multiple reporting periods or have there been discrepancies between the tax rates. Should a business be report lower tax rate, its earnings may appear to have increased however they have actually remained constant and a higher net income is only attributable to tax differences.
- **Inventory & Accounts Receivable**: Should the business be reporting a build-up in inventory or accounts receivable this may be a warning sign that there that the firm is unable to sell its products or appropriately bill its clients. Such a build-up may distort the firm's asset position as it appears that the firm assets have a higher value than they do in reality.
- **Quality of investments/regulatory risks**: Investments made in marketable securities (shares/bonds) may be listed by the firm at the acquired price, however the actual market value may differ significantly from the original purchase price. Similarly, the regulations governing certain industries such as Banking, Oil & Gas may change significantly over time. It is important that management accurately presents the impact of these changes on the firm.

Company Investment activities

A firm's investment activities are its investments in buying or selling assets. The Cash flow statement will show you the amount of money received or spent by a firm from its investment activities. The two main long-term investments which firms make are fixed asset investments and equity investments. Here are some examples of business investment activities:

- Property, Buildings or land rights
- Machinery, Equipment, stationary or tools.
- Trading securities, bonds, cash equivalents
- Cash paid to acquire intellectual property, patents or an acquisition of an additional business unit through a merger and acquisition.

Why are investment activities important?

A company's investment activities are extremely important as they illustrate how a firm is allocating its capital and choosing to invest the surplus funds from its business. Firm's which are continually required to renew leases, purchase property rights and equipment may have extremely high capital expenditures which require extensive cash outlay just for the firm to remain competitive. Without firm undertaking extensive capital expenditures, in a very capital intensive industry, it may risk losing its competitive advantage and become threatened by the competition.

Firm's pursuing mergers and acquisitions are those which are pursuing non-organic growth strategies. This also poses significant business risk as it deviates substantially from a company's core competencies and involves taking on an entirely new management team. Investors therefore regularly screen a firm's past history of acquisitions and bolt-on business purchases, to assess the quality of a management's judgement in choosing to acquire other businesses and how they are using surplus capital.

On the other hand, firm's which engage in significant trade activities and purchase significant numbers of securities, long and short-term bonds may be generating significant free cash flow.

Investors must screen the quality of a firm's trade activities in order to understand how efficiently a firm is investing its surplus capital. Firm's which engage in significant trade activities may also be located in an industry where this is generally expected or they are required to trade heavily in order to maintain the competitive position. Examples of this include the insurance industry, banks and financial services.

Businesses operating activities

Businesses operating activities are the primary activities of a business. Operating Income reflects a business's income from its core operating activities relating to its product or service offerings. Businesses operating activities will determine whether or not a firm is ultimately successful and whether or not growth in the industry is sustainable for the business.

A business's profitability from its operating activities can be found on the cash flow statement, under the section cash flows from operating activities. Investors consider the cash flows which a firm is generating from its primary operating activities to be crucial as this reflects where a business is generating its income from. Investors consider it particularly important that there exists a consistency and predictability about the income that a firm is generating and that the firm has a proven track record of generating cash flow. The quality of a firm's cash flow is therefore crucial and it is important that funds are being generated from recurring sources rather than as a result of once off events such as the sale of assets.

Analysing a firm's operating activities also has several key advantages:

The amount of depreciation and amortization being charged: This enables investors to evaluate how capital intensive a businesses' operating activities and the structure of its operations. This can be particularly crucial in sectors such as the pharmaceutical sector and the oil and gas industry.

The success of its investing activities: Firm's may rely heavily on their investments to generate income. This is reflected on the business's cash flow from operating activities statement and may serve as a useful reference point for predicting future free cash flow.

The impact of foreign exchange rates: Firm's which generate a large proportion of their revenue from overseas will regularly be impacted by changes in foreign exchange rates. Analysing the firm's cash flow statement will generally provide a useful benchmark to review what has taken place within the business year and what is likely to take place in the future.

Taxes payable, salaries payable and accounts payable: This provides crucial insight into the capital structure of the business and how it has structured its business to go forward.

Gross Margins

A company's gross margin is the percentage that remains after subtracting the direct costs of a product or service production from revenue. Gross margins can be calculated using the following formula:

Revenue-COGS/Revenue

For example, if a firm's revenue is $1 million dollars and cost of goods $300,000. It can be calculated that the firm's gross margin is 70%.

High gross margins (above 40%) reflect greater levels of production efficiency and are considered desirable by most companies. It reflects that a company is able to deliver products to a consumer at a lower cost and a durable competitive advantage. Robust gross margins reflect that the company is able to effectively leverage its production capabilities and minimize both fixed and variable costs which impact the profitability of the sale such as raw materials and shipping costs. Gross margins are considered to be reflective of the company's core profitability as they cannot be reduced in the same way as operating expenses can be cut.

Gross margins in Practice

Companies that have high gross margins are also considered to be less vulnerable to downturns in the economic cycle as they are able to preserve levels of profitability and compete effectively on price.

Michael Porter reflects that firms who are able to maintain consistently high gross margins may be operating in more favourable industries than firms who are consistently unable to raise their gross margins. Firms who have low gross margins may be in industries where customers have low levels of consumer loyalty, high bargaining power and intense competitive rivalry. Such firms may see their gross profits deteriorate as a result of inflationary pressures which can raise their cost of sales. They may have to pass these price increases onto consumers, which ultimately threatens market share. For start-up businesses, analysing gross margins can aid investors in analysing which business sectors are achieving the highest levels of profitably to focus on maximizing returns. It can also be used to benchmark against competitors or set price targets.

Analysing gross margins is crucial for evaluating a business's pricing power and ability to sustain (grow) profit margins organically over time. It is important to note that the industry in which a company operates has the greatest effect on its profits margins.

Company intangible assets

Intangible assets are items which are non-physical in nature. They cannot physically be 'touched' and have useful lives of longer than one year. However, despite the fact that intangible assets don't have a physical value, they are often considered even more valuable than tangible assets. Examples of intangible assets include:

- **Brands:** These are indefinite in nature and are a major factor in determining the company's success. It is clear that the brand power of companies such as Apple, Amazon or Coca-Cola, is a major driving source of sales as these firms obtain brand-name recognition and are widely known by consumers.
- **Goodwill:** This refers to the ongoing positive relationships that a firm may have built with its clients, distributors or business partners, which enables them to obtain ongoing business.
- **Patents**: These are usually used by pharmaceutical companies or technology companies and protect the firm from having its inventions copied or appropriated by other firms. Patents may assist in protecting a firm's monopoly in specific sector and ensure a durable competitive advantage.
- **Trademarks**: Trademarks are symbols or words associated with a company that are legally registered. This includes, for example the 'Apple symbol' associated with Apple computers or the 'Swoosh' associated with Nike shoes.
- **Copyrights**: These are legal rights to print, publish or distribute musical or artistic work by the creator of an item. Audio, drawings and software may all be copyrighted and have distribution exclusivity.

Drawing value from intangible assets

The reason that intangible assets can be more valuable than physical assets is that a company does not have to continually pay repairs or maintenance associated with the upkeep, in the way that it is required incurs expenditure with tangible assets. The ability of a business to command a premium as a result of its brand name or intellectual property may enable it to sustain higher profit margins than competitors over time. It may also reflect a company's skill or expertise in a particular area as it is able to continually generate intangible assets which generate profits for the business.

A firm which has intangible assets can profit from having a favourable reputation and allowing the 'value' of their product to determine the ultimate selling price rather than the cost of production.

Company operating cash flow?

A company's operating cash flow is the amount of cash which has been generated from its regular business operations. This serves as an excellent measure of the performance of the company's core business strength and how it is evolving over time. The company's operating cash flow is vital as it represents a company's ability to generate profitability, fund expansion and capital expenditures and purchase inventory going forward.

A company which is generating significant operating cash flow, usually also does not need to incur large amounts of debt as it has enough free cash flow to support its business requirements. Here are some crucial factors to understanding operating cash flow:

Operating cash-flow includes various non-cash charges which are not counted in terms of calculating net income. This includes stock-based compensation, depreciation & amortization and other expenses.

Operating cash flows concentrate on cash generated by a company's main business activities. This includes selling and purchasing inventory or changes in the value of the inventory. Operating cash flows are also generated by the company's investments and accounts payable.

Importance of Operating Cash flow

There are a number of fundamental reasons why operating cash flow is extremely important in terms of calculating a firm's intrinsic earning power. These include:

Removing accounting charges which do not accurately represent the earning power of a business. For example, adding back depreciation and amortisation helps to provide a more accurate depiction of the quality of business operations.

Removing extraordinary earnings/losses. These are not representative of the normalised earning power of a firm and may distort the firm's net income for a given period, providing an inaccurate analysis of the business. As operating earnings measure the firm's recurring income, investors can have confidence in the ability of a firm to continue to generate significant amounts of cash flow in the future.

Comparing revenue generated to expenses incurred. This enables a clearer picture to be developed regarding how the firm is able to generate free cash flow, which can then be distributed to shareholders.

When operating cash flow is analysed in conjunction with the firms investing and financing activities, a more complete picture is able to work out how the business will evolve over time. Additionally, referring to the discussion from management provides more precise insight than simply looking at the income generated.

A company's interest coverage ratio

A firm's interest coverage ratio reflects how easily the firm can service its interest expenses on its outstanding debt. A high interest coverage ratio means the firm can comfortably service its debt, while a lower ratio means it is under greater pressure to meet repayments. The interest coverage ratio is calculated using the following formula:

Earnings before interest and taxes/ interest expense

The amount of debt which a firm should generally take on and the 'acceptable' interest coverage ratio depends on a number of crucial factors. These include:

- The cyclical nature of the industry: Firms which operate in industries that are highly cyclical, for example the auto-industry/industrial goods may have a harder time serving their short-term debt during times of sustained economic downturn. Consequently, it is generally advisable that these firms take on lower levels of debt and have more manageable interest coverage ratios.
- The industry in which the firm operates: Certain industries such as the oil & gas sector have very high costs at the beginning, which gradually decrease as operations are set up. This is because large costs are often incurred with exploration, pipelines built for transport and opening refineries. However, costs decrease dramatically once operations are in 'full swing'. For these firms the interest coverage ratio generally starts off low and increases gradually.
- The size of the firm: Larger firms do not generally require large amounts of debt to grow their operations. They usually have large cash reserves/are generating regular cash flow. Larger firms are also usually at a more mature stage in the business cycle. On the other hand, smaller firms may require taking on larger amounts of debt to promote their products and grow their business. Borrowing rates may also be higher for smaller firms. As a consequence their interest coverage ratios may be higher and gradually decrease over time.

It is crucial for a firm to meet its short-term borrowing obligations. Not being able to service its debt may even put a very high quality firm out of business, simply as a result of a short-term downturn. It is therefore crucial to undertake an in-depth analysis of the firm's interest coverage ratio and determine whether or not it is appropriate, depending on the sector it operates/the requirements and size of the firm.

"Take one simple idea and take it seriously."

Charlie Munger

Chapter 9: Company management and capital allocation

Despite being a direct factor of long-term investor returns, few investors actually focus on identifying management teams that allocate capital well. The "holy grail" in investing is to find an **excellent monopoly business, trading at a discount to fair value with a management team that allocates capital well.**

Why Capital Allocation Matters:

Management teams have a basic toolbox of decisions they can make to generate returns. The equation itself is relatively straightforward. First, capital can be obtained in four ways, the sale of debt, the sale of equity, the sale of assets and through internally generated operating cash flow. Next, the capital can be allocated in five different ways, either the issuance of dividends, the repurchase of stock, the retirement of debt, the purchase of other assets (M&A) or the reinvestment back into the business (i.e. Capex or net working capital additions.)

Among each of these decisions, no specific one has precedence over the others. This is a critical concept that few investors or management teams truly appreciate. Whether capital is obtained through issuing debt or through operating cash flow, the capital is still finite and should be treated as such. A common misconception that many management teams and investors have is their view that operating cash flow is free and costless. This is not true as its real cost is the opportunity cost of other projects that could be done with the cash. Investors have been and should be upset when a management team uses operating cash flow to spend it on new internal projects with poor prospects of sufficient returns.

Lastly, the question of capital allocation is not cut and dry. The best answer a management team could give investors regarding their view on capital allocation is: "it depends." A common answer by some management teams might be to first spend on the business itself (new Capex or R&D) then pay a dividend and then use the rest of the excess capital for share repurchases. The graph below depicts this concept as share repurchases tend to peak during cyclical economic peaks, when operating cash flows are at their highest levels.

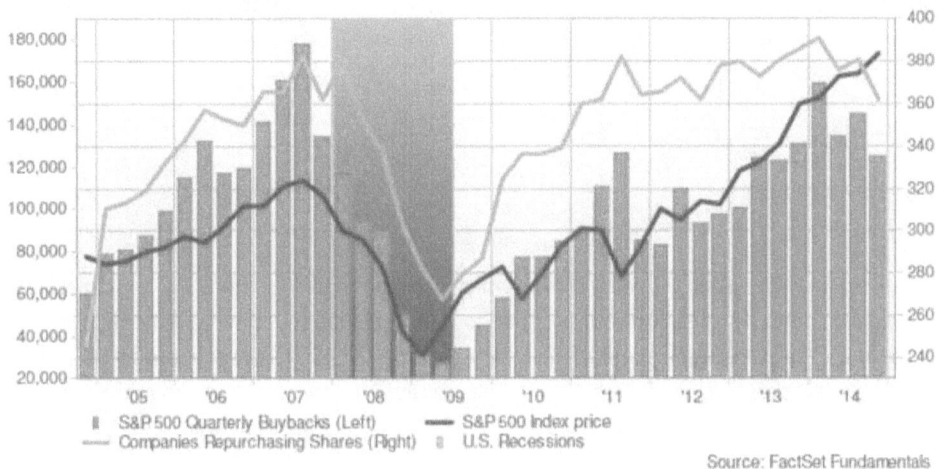

Source: FactSet fundamentals

This decision process is flawed, however, because capital should be allocated towards its next highest return. When a business is earning very high returns in its core business, reinvestment makes sense but if incremental returns are slowing, the company should not spend more despite the prospects of the business growing future revenues and profits. If the share price is substantially undervalued, the company should forego cash dividends and instead repurchase stock. If the share price is extremely expensive, M&A multiples far too high and all reinvestment opportunities exhausted, the last resort for management should be to pay a special cash dividend. This kind of flexibility in decision making may make investors nervous or less likely to buy a stock but it is the correct mindset for management teams who wish to drive attractive long-term shareholder returns.

Finding Management Teams with Good Capital Allocation Skills:

How does one find which management teams are apt at capital allocation? First, assess how a company's management team discusses and presents its view on capital allocation. Does management think growth in the business should come at all costs? Are they beholden to a cash dividend no matter what other options for capital allocation exist? Do they not have an internal hurdle rate for returns when they do an M&A transaction? These types of viewpoints are indicative of a management team that does not have a solid grasp on proper capital allocation.

Good management teams will describe the financial reasoning for their decisions. For example, for an M&A transaction, mentioning of the multiple to EBITDA or cash flow and how the deal is accretive to EPS and attractive on an ROIC basis are all needed to be sure the management team is doing due diligence. If a company is making share repurchases, they should make mention of their view on how undervalued the shares are. If the company is making share repurchases no matter what the multiple of the stock is to EPS or FCF, that is a telltale sign that management isn't focused on capital allocation.

Investors should be very wary of management teams and their capital allocation skills. Many CEOs move up through a company in divisions that don't train them in proper capital allocation, leaving them less than apt at making investors above average shareholder returns. By staying focused on how management teams allocate capital, investors can figure out whether their investments' management teams are making capital allocation decisions that maximize future shareholder returns.

How Management teams can deploy capital?

Organic Reinvestment

Organic reinvestment is likely the most simple and straightforward form of capital allocation. Instead of diverting funds away from a core business line to make balance sheet improvements, perform acquisitions, or return capital to shareholders, managers opt to reinvest excess capital into the operating business that originally generated it. The decision on whether or not to reinvest funds is completely dependent on two factors:

Capacity: How much capital can reasonably be reinvested per unit of time before diminishing returns occur

Business Unit Profitability: Generally measured by return on invested capital, this shows the return that can be expected on any reinvested capital

Business unit leaders can proxy the returns from organic reinvestment by multiplying their reinvestment rate by the business' return on capital. So if a business reinvests 50% of capital at a 20% ROIC, then a 10% incremental return can be reasonably expected.

It is important to keep in mind that many businesses *have no choice* about whether or not to reinvest.

- It generates excess free cash flow that can be invested elsewhere
- Its competitive position is strong and unlikely to deteriorate in the near future
- Again, Berkshire Hathaway is a phenomenal example of a company that sometimes purchases slow-growing businesses because of their ability to generate high levels of excess cash flows that can be reinvested in other growth projects.

In fact, Warren Buffett once warned about the perils of mindlessly investing money back into the company that generated it:

"Long-term competitive advantage in a stable industry is what we seek in a business. If that comes with rapid organic growth, great. But even without organic growth, such a business is rewarding. We will simply take the lush earnings of the business and use them to buy similar businesses elsewhere. There's no rule that you have to invest money where you've earned it. Indeed, it's often a mistake to do so: Truly great businesses, earning huge returns on tangible assets, can't for any extended period reinvest a large portion of their earnings internally at high rates of return." – Warren Buffett in Berkshire Hathaway's 2007 Annual Report

Share Repurchases

Share repurchases are likely the most misunderstood capital allocation policy adopted by corporate managers. They are also one of the most powerful if executed properly. Share repurchases occur when a company buys back *its own shares*, reducing the number of shares outstanding. This has the beneficial effect of improving important per-share financial metrics such as earnings-per-share, book-value-per-share, and free-cash-flow-per-share. With that said, the impact of share repurchases is *completely dependent* on the price that the company pays for its shares. Ideally, a company will buy back its stock when it trades at low valuations (based on multiples of earnings, book value, or cash flow), and cease buybacks when valuations rise.

To understand why the price of repurchased shares is important, consider the following quote from Berkshire Hathaway's 2016 Annual Report:

"Consider a simple analogy: If there are three equal partners in a business worth $3,000 and one is bought out by the partnership for $900, each of the remaining partners realizes an immediate gain of $50. If the exiting partner is paid $1,100, however, the continuing partners each suffer a loss of $50. The same math applies with corporations and their shareholders. Ergo, the question of whether a repurchase action is value-enhancing or value-destroying for continuing shareholders is entirely purchase-price dependent."

— Warren Buffett in Berkshire Hathaway's 2016 Annual Report

But what if the company is short on cash, and cannot fund a meaningful share repurchase program? Buybacks financed with debt have the potential to build tremendous shareholder value. This is particularly true if interest rates are low *and* if the company pays a dividend. Repurchasing dividend stocks is more meaningful than repurchasing non-dividend stocks because of the future savings that result from paying less in dividends on a reduced share count. In addition, the tax deductibility of interest payments means that even if the additional interest expense is slightly higher than the dividend savings, the corporation may be slightly better off on an after-tax basis. For an illustration of this, consider Apple's current capital return program, which – at $300 billion – is impressive in both magnitude and execution. Apple currently pays approximately 1.9%, on average, on its newly issued debt. The company's dividend yield is 1.7% – lower than its current interest rate – but Apple *still saves money* from repurchasing stock because of the tax deductibility of interest expenses.

A walkthrough of the mathematics behind Apple's buyback is shown below.

The Cost Savings of Apple's Share Repurchase Program

Amount spent on buybacks	$	1,000.0
Additional interest expense	$	(19.0)
Add back: Tax savings	$	4.9 (26% of $19)
Add back: Dividend savings	$	17.0
Net savings:	$	2.9

Note: assumes 1.7% dividend yield, 26% effective tax rate, and 1.9% weighted average interest rate

Apple's share repurchase program is one example of very intelligent capital allocation. They are not the only company to buyback stock using cheap debt and benefitting from the interest savings – Philip Morris (PM) has implemented a similar strategy in the past.

All said, share repurchases have the potential to build tremendous shareholder value *if* they are executed at a price below intrinsic value. Companies that can repurchase their high yield common shares using cheap debt magnify the benefits of this capital allocation strategy.

"Mimicking the herd invites regression to the mean (merely average performance)."

Charles T Munger

Chapter 9: How to value a monopoly business

In the 1987 shareholder letter to GEICO stockholders, Lou Simpson, one of the most successful investors of all time, described what he looked for in a potential investment. They included "Think independently", "Invest in high-return businesses run for shareholders," "Pay only a reasonable price, even for an excellent business," "Invest for the long-term," and "Do not diversify excessively. "

He also mentioned a concept that we have only briefly touched upon and that is the long-term treasury yield and how it has important implications for the valuation you should use to determine the relative attractiveness of a company.

Long-Term Treasury Bonds

As humans, we have a deep need for benchmarks; standards against which all other things must be measured. On Wall Street, everything gets compared to long-term Treasury bond yields. These bonds, issued by the Federal Government to raise funds for day-to-day operating needs, are considered the "risk-free" rate because there is no reasonable chance of default. Why? Congress has the power to tax.

If the government were unable to meet its obligations, our representatives on Capitol Hill would merely need to jack up tax revenues. (Of course, in such a situation, inflation may have begun to run rampant meaning that although you would get your money back, the actual value of those dollars as measured in terms of how many hamburgers or boxes of laundry detergent you could buy would be worth far less.)

At the time of this book, the 30-year Treasury yields 2.82%. The theory behind this benchmark is that every investor in the world should ask himself (or herself) first and foremost: "If I can earn 2.82% on my money without taking any risk, what premium should I demand for riskier assets such as stocks?"

Of course, most people don't actually pose the question to themselves this way. Instead, they may look at shares of Coca-Cola and determine that at a price-to-earnings ratio of 23 (which means an earnings yield of 4.34%) they aren't willing to invest .Or, they may conclude that Coke has growth prospects – whereas the treasury does not – and it has the ability to weather a storm in the event of widespread inflation. People are still going to drink soda, even in the midst of a great depression because it is, as the company has pointed out, an "affordable luxury."

For you as an investor, you need to determine the **relative yield of any investment vs Treasury Bills** and access the ability of the company's earnings to grow, in addition to the risk you are taking with the investment. **Ideally, you should look for a company with high growth prospects, the potential to grow earnings and have it operate in a low risk, consolidated industry.**

Chapter 10: Assessing profitability growth through industry relevant metrics

You will notice that an industry begins to consolidate when there is an improvement in industry specific metrics. These metrics are the reference point for any investor who is looking to make an investment into a consolidated industry. What are some examples of industry relevant metrics?

- **Revenue ton miles for railroads**: The amount of revenue each railway earns for every ton of cargo it transports. As you might imagine, if the cargo that a railway is transporting becomes more valuable relative to the distance travelled, earnings go up immensely. This is exactly what happened in the American railway industry after it consolidated.
- **Revenue passenger miles for airlines**: This is the amount of revenue earned per passenger for every mile travelled. Again, as you might imagine, if an airline can consistently earn more money for every mile travelled from its customers, profitability will go right up. Again, this was the case in the airline industry.
- **Market share for cigarette manufactures**: Given the regulatory burdens on cigarette manufacturing, it became almost impossible for new entrants to break into the market. As consolidation took place, leading brands such as Marlboro have continued to gain market share while competitors have dropped off. For the astute investor, he can recognize this as being an effective monopoly and profit from it.
- **Regulation for rating agencies**: For credit rating agencies such as Moody's it was noticeable that there was an consistent improvement in the company's performance, year on year as the regulation which was attached to credit ratings became more burdensome and enshrined in legislation. This lead to a massive improvement in performance metrics.

For the smart investor, recognizing industry consolidation begins by identifying changing patterns in the most important industry metrics. If you can see that the shape of a particular industry changing in a favourable manner, it is probably time to start taking a closer look.

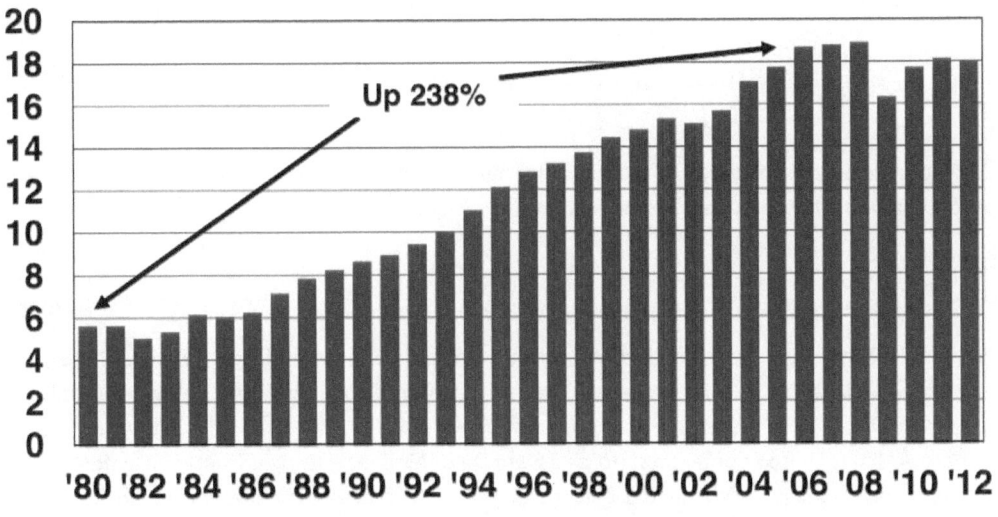

(millions of revenue ton-miles per mile of railroad)

Up 238%

Miles = route-miles owned   Data are for Class I railroads.   Source: AAR

Figure 1: Showing how Revenue passenger miles increased, as the railroad industry consolidated

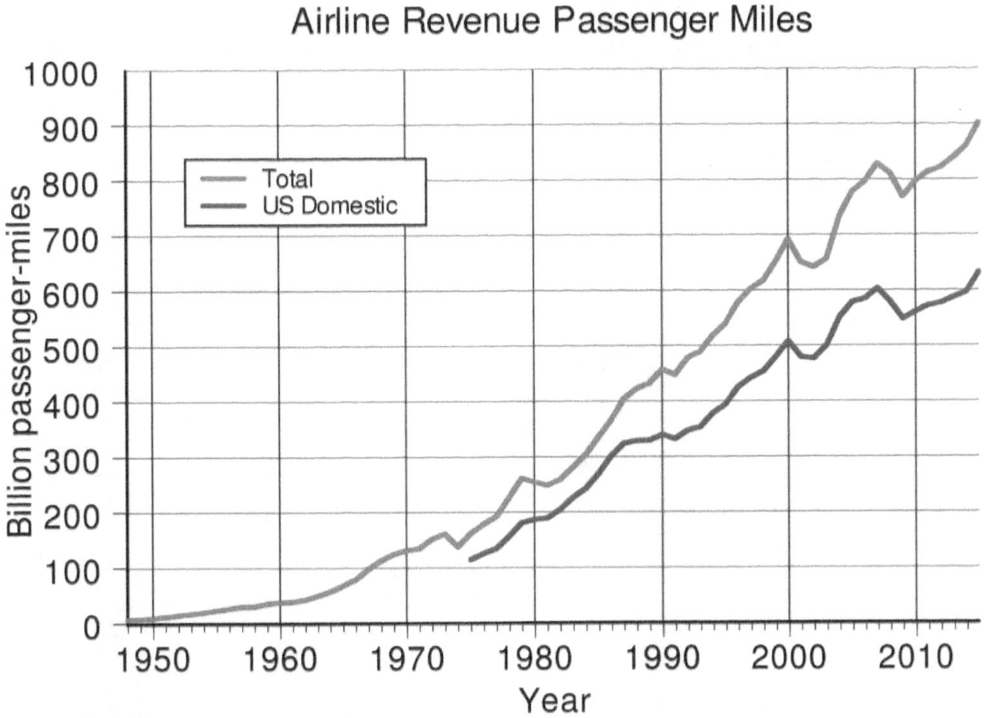

Airline Revenue Passenger Miles

Figure 2: How Airline revenue passenger miles have improved with deregulation

"Most people are too fretful, they worry too much. Success means being very patient, but aggressive when it's time." Charlie Munger

Chapter 11: Case studies in Consolidation

This chapter seeks to provide you a **practical illustration of how industries have consolidated over time and how this has impacted investment in the sector.**

The Airline Industry

Having made heavy losses over the last several decades, the US airline industry has always been considered as a laggard by active investors. The sector suffered combined losses of over $52 billion between 1977 to 2009. Further, the economic slowdown in 2009-2010 forced the legacy carriers – American Airlines, United Continental Holdings and Delta Air lines – to significantly slash down their capacity to match the lower demand for air travel. While the recession further magnified the losses of the airlines, these legacy carriers continued to follow capacity discipline even after the air travel demand improved post 2010. Although this enabled the airlines to raise the air fares, and reduce their losses, it wasn't sufficient to pull the industry out of its heavy losses. Consequently, a number of airlines were pushed into bankruptcy post the slowdown, resulting in a number of mergers and acquisitions over the last decade. Below we show some of the most significant mergers that have materialized over the last decade and changed the dynamics of the industry. For instance, Continental Airlines merged with United Airlines in 2010 and US Airways merged with American Airlines in 2013 to bail the latter out of its bankruptcy.

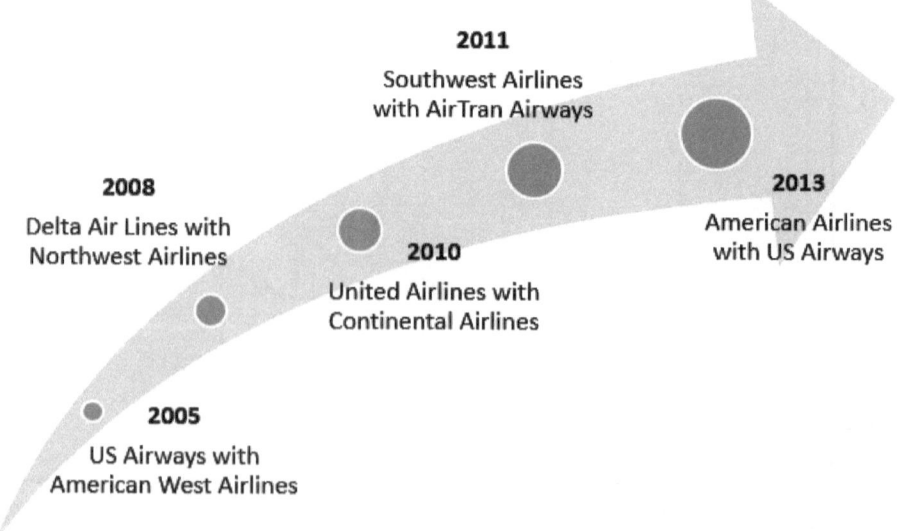

Apart from pulling out the airlines from bankruptcy, these deals were instrumental in changing the landscape of the US airline industry. These mergers resulted in the consolidation of capacity with the top 4 US airlines in the industry, namely American, United, Delta, and Southwest Airlines. At present, these airlines hold almost 85% of the market share, as opposed to only 65% share (on average) held by the top 4 US airlines in the past. As a result, these airlines currently operate as an informal oligopoly and control the dynamics of the overall air travel market, even though the sector is monitored by a number of regulatory bodies.

US Airline Industry	1990	2000	2010	2015
Top 4 Airlines	- American Airlines - Delta Air Lines - US Airways - United Airlines	- American Airlines - Delta Air Lines - Northwest Airlines - United Airlines	- American Airlines - Delta Air Lines - Southwest Airlines - United Continental	- American Airlines - Delta Air Lines - Southwest Airlines - United Continental
Combined Market Share	68%	61%	65%	84%

The tobacco Industry

Since facing a wave of litigation in the 1980s and '90s over the health consequences of smoking, tobacco companies have sought to reposition themselves through mergers and acquisitions. Some tobacco companies — like R.J. Reynolds, which bought Nabisco Brands in 1985 — have sought to diversify into additional businesses. Others, like Japan Tobacco, have hunted for expansion opportunities overseas. As cigarette sales continued to fall in the late 1990s and 2000s, some companies got out of the tobacco business entirely. Nabisco broke apart from Reynolds, and the Loews Corporation shed Lorillard.

Below is a selected history of tobacco deal-making over the last three decades.

1988: RJR Nabisco buyout | In a deal that riveted Wall Street and set a new record for leveraged buyouts, Kohlberg Kravis Roberts paid $30.2 billion for RJR Nabisco, a tobacco and packaged food giant that had been formed in a merger just a few years earlier. The deal was a signature deal for K.K.R. — it was recounted in the classic book "Barbarians at the Gate" — but the buyout firm ended up with a lackluster return on its investment.

1999: Rothmans acquisition | the cigarette business was racing to consolidate in the late 1990s, as it battled lawsuits. Rothmans International, a British tobacco company, was acquired by British American Tobacco in 1999 for $7.5 billion. Rothmans had grown through a series of deals in the 1990s and was controlled by South Africa's billionaire Rupert family. The British American Tobacco deal brought together the second- and fourth-largest tobacco companies in the world, creating a formidable rival to Philip Morris.

1999: RJR's sale to the Japanese | The food and tobacco empire of RJR Nabisco broke apart when the company sold its international tobacco business to Japan Tobacco for $7.8 billion. Soon afterward, in a transaction that officially separated the two halves of the company, RJR's domestic tobacco business was spun off to shareholders and renamed R.J. Reynolds Tobacco Holdings.

2006: Another Japanese deal | Japan Tobacco bought Gallaher Group, a British cigarette maker, for $18.8 billion. The deal, which at the time was the biggest ever overseas acquisition by a Japanese company, was intended to help Japan Tobacco expand outside its home market, where smoking had declined.

2007: Imperial Tobacco's big deal | The Imperial Tobacco Group, the British maker of Davidoff cigarettes and Rizla rolling papers, bought Altadis of Spain for $21.5 billion, gaining Gauloises cigarettes and Cohiba cigars. It was the biggest tobacco acquisition in Europe, signaling Imperial Tobacco's ambitions to expand beyond Britain, where antismoking measures were hurting business.

2007: The Loews separation from Lorillard | The Loews Corporation, a conglomerate whose holdings included the hotel chain bearing its name, finally shed its interest in Lorillard Tobacco, after years of reducing its stake. The $8.3 billion deal, structured as a spinoff to shareholders, was a sign of the times. Tobacco, said Ben Bornstein, an analyst at Omega Advisors, "is not a pleasant business to be in."

2008: Altria's smokeless deal | The Altria Group, which had formerly been known as Philip Morris, bought UST, the maker of Skoal and Copenhagen smokeless tobacco, for $11.6 billion. The deal was Altria's first major acquisition since spinning off its international tobacco business in March 2008, and it was meant to capitalize on the growing popularity of smokeless tobacco, especially as sales of traditional cigarettes were declining.

As you can see, this wave of consolidation has made the industry more monopolistic than ever.

Natural Monopolies

In some rarer circumstances, an industry may consolidate naturally. This takes place without massive consolidation, but rather the emergence of one company which naturally dominates an industry. This has taken place with companies like Facebook, Amazon, Google and Netflix. If you can find a natural monopoly, even better!

"People calculate too much and think too little."

Charles T Munger

Chapter 13: Maintaining Investment discipline and profiting from Consolidation

As a rule, you should buy stocks with the intention of holding them for a long, long time, meaning at least ten years and perhaps forever. The reason is simple: Deciding to buy something is hard enough, but deciding to sell is even harder. You have to know what to sell, when to sell and what to replace it with. Plus, once you own a stock, your emotions, not just your money, are invested in it. You may become reluctant to sell an overpriced winner that's lost its competitive edge because it has been so good to you. Or you may hesitate to dump a troubled loser because doing so would confirm your stupidity. So make limited buying decisions and hardly any selling decisions. As Warren Buffett once put it, "Inactivity strikes us as intelligent behaviour."

Most investors leave and enter stocks with way too much frequency.

Sell because something has changed for the worse. In Common Stocks and Uncommon Profits, one of the best investing books ever published, Philip Fisher wrote, "It is only occasionally that there is any reason for selling at all." That occasional reason is "the deterioration of a company's underlying business." In Fisher's view, there were only two possible causes of a deteriorating condition: bad management (which usually meant a change at the top wasn't working out) or decreased prospects for a company's products. As my wife is fond of saying, this seems to be an insight into the obvious.

There are only three reasons you should sell a stock:

Wrong Facts: There are times after a security is purchased that the investor realizes the facts do not support the supposed rosy reasons of the original purchase. If the purchase thesis was initially built on a shaky foundation, then the shares should be sold.

Changing Facts: The facts of the original purchase may have been deemed correct, but facts can change negatively over the passage of time. Management deterioration and/or the exhaustion of growth opportunities are a few reasons why a security should be sold according to Fisher.

Scarcity of Cash: If there is a shortage of cash available, and if a unique opportunity presents itself, then Fisher advises the sale of other securities to fund the purchase.

Many investors are reactive and sell at the same time everyone else does—when they're fearful. But your emotions aren't the best guide for making critical financial decisions.

> "It takes character to sit with all that cash and to do nothing.
> I didn't get top where I am by going after mediocre opportunities."
>
> Charlie Munger

Chapter 14: Choosing an Investment vehicle that fits your lifestyle

If your goal is not to be a professional investor it might be a good idea for you to look for a managed fund to invest in. With so many funds out there, it can be difficult to know exactly what you should look for when selecting a managed fund. Here are some key pointers to consider.

Low Performance Fees

You need to achieve maximum return possible as an investor. If you have an investment manager who charges you exorbitant fees, this will eat away at your earnings. Selecting a manager who has a reasonable fee structure will put more money in your pocket over the entire investment period.

No/low management fees

Like performance fees above, whatever fund you invest in, should have a manageable level of management fees. Some funds charge 1 to 2 percent of the invested capital in management fees. I don't believe this is the right way to do it. Such high management fees eat away at investor's capital and simply act as a drag on performance. I recommend selecting firm's which charge low management fees.

Proven Track Record

While the past is not a perfect predictor of the future, investment managers past performance can give you a good insight. For example, if you had seen Warren Buffett's record with his investment partnerships you may have been able to follow him into Berkshire Hathaway, which would have a pretty good idea.

Methodology

All investment is fundamentally value driven. Your investment manager needs to be buying companies for less than what they are worth. For you as a partner in his investment company you need to full understand how your manager is selecting invests. If you are confident about his investment methodology then you will have confidence riding out the tough times with him.

Chapter 15: Takeaways from this book

Looking for monopoly businesses is one of the most underappreciated investment approaches. Investing in these kind of industries, reduces unforced investment errors and provides investors with the certainty they require to achieve. It is one of the keys to my investment success

If you are interested in learning more feel free to contact me at mpinto@intelfunds.com if you are interested in investing with me, please do not hesitate to contact me either to learn more. Feel free to also checkout my website at www.intelfunds.com

www.ingramcontent.com/pod-product-compliance
Lightning Source LLC
Chambersburg PA
CBHW030519220526
45464CB00006B/2871